STARTING GEOGRAPHY

Landscapes

Written by
Helen Barden

Illustrated by
Robert Wheeler

Wayland

Books in the series

Clothes and Costumes
Conservation
Houses and Homes
Journeys
Landscapes
Resources
Water
Weather and Climate

This edition published in 1994 by
Wayland (Publishers) Ltd

First published in 1992 by
Wayland (Publishers) Ltd
61 Western Road, Hove
East Sussex, BN3 1JD, England

Series editor: Mandy Suhr
Designer: Jean Wheeler
Consultants: Julie Warne and Lorraine Harrison

British Library Cataloguing in Publication Data

Barden, Helen
Landscapes.–(Starting geography)
I. Title II. Series
910

HARDBACK ISBN 0-7502-0454-0

PAPERBACK ISBN 0-7502-0612-8

Typeset by DP Press, Sevenoaks, Kent
Printed in Italy by Rotolito Lombarda, S.p.A., Milan

Contents

Looking at the land 4
Mountains in the clouds 6
Smaller mountains 8
Up the hills and down the slopes 10
Valleys 12
Flowing water 14
Lakes and waterfalls 16
Exploring the coastline 18
Lots of sand 20
Plains 22
Changing the landscape 24
Building new landscapes 26
Landscapes for the future 28

Glossary 30
Books to read 31
Index 32

The words printed in **bold** are explained in the glossary.

Looking at the land

Look around you, what do you see? The land is shaped in many different ways. There are mountains and hills, valleys and rivers, deserts and plains, seas and coastlines.

All these together make up the **landscape** in which we live.

The shape of the land is changing all the time. Most natural changes happen very slowly over millions of years.

People can also make changes to the landscape when they do things like building new houses and roads.

Activity

What kind of landscape can you see near your home?

Mountains in the clouds

▲ Mountains are made of very hard rock. They are usually a pointed shape and have very steep sides. This mountain is called K2. It is in Pakistan.

Some mountains are so high that the tops are above the clouds and covered with snow all year. The highest part of a mountain is called the **peak**.

The ground nearest the peak of the mountain is mostly rocky and bare because plants find it difficult to grow there. It is too cold near the top for most animals to survive.

This mountain yak has a thick coat to protect it from the cold. ▶

People are able to live lower down the mountain. These people from the Himalayas live in houses with thick walls to help to keep them warm. ▼

Smaller mountains

▲ These mountains are called the Alps. They are smaller mountains. Trees and grass can grow on the lower slopes.

◀ Farmers often keep sheep and goats on the mountainside. These animals can climb the rocky hillside easily. They feed on the grass and other plants that grow there.

▲ In winter, the mountains are covered with heavy snow. Many people go on holiday to the Alps to ski down the snowy slopes. Ski lifts have been built to make getting to the higher parts of the mountain easier.

Make a model of a mountain from papier mâché. Can you build a model ski lift too?

During the summer, some people like to climb the **face** of the mountain. Others explore the mountain paths. Have you ever been up a mountain?

Up the hills and down the slopes

▲ Hills are **mounds** of earth and rock. They can be large with long sloping sides, or just small bumps in the ground. Hills are not as high as mountains.

The tops of hills are usually rounded and the sides are not so steep as those of mountains. Sometimes you may see a single hill, but quite often they are in long lines.

▲ Plants usually grow easily on the hillsides and some are covered with forests. The gentle slopes of hills make good grazing land for sheep and cows.

Have you ever run down the slope of a hill or flown a kite from the top? Maybe you have walked over hills and followed a path along the **ridge**.

Valleys

A valley is a long **channel** in the land. The bottom of a valley may be flat. The sides may be steep hills or more gentle slopes.

◀ Some valleys are made by rivers and streams. Over many years, the flowing water slowly wears away the rocks and soil, making a groove for the water to flow along.

Sometimes valleys have been made by huge cracks in the earth's surface, or by ice moving down from the mountains hundreds of years ago.

Lots of people choose to live along a valley floor. The soil here is usually very good for growing crops and there is plenty of grass for animals like dairy cows.

Flowing water

When rain falls on the land, it flows downhill to form rivers and streams. Some water may also come from ice melting in the mountains.

Rivers gradually change the shape of the land. The moving water wears away rocks and soil as it finds a path to the sea. Some rivers are so long that they flow through several countries, like the River Rhine in Europe, shown in the picture above. Others are so wide that you cannot see across them, like parts of the Mississippi River in the USA.

Find a river on a large-scale map. Can you trace its path?

Rivers can be used like a busy road. They carry boats of all sizes up and down on their journeys. This river is in Thailand.
Have you been on a boat down a river? ▼

Lakes and waterfalls

Lakes are formed when water fills a **hollow** in the land. The water may come from rain or from a **spring** deep underground. Most lakes contain fresh water.

Some lakes have been formed by building a dam across a river. A dam is a very strong wall that holds back the water to make a reservoir. A reservoir is a lake made by people to store water. We use the water for things like drinking and washing. ▶

This lake is in Canada which is famous for its great lakes.

Waterfalls are caused by water tumbling down over a cliff. This picture shows the famous Niagara Falls that form part of the **boundary** between Canada and the USA.

Exploring the coastline

Our planet Earth is made of water and land. A coastline or beach is where the sea meets the land.

◀ Some beaches have palm trees and golden sand, like this beach in the Caribbean. Others have steep cliffs and rocks or pebbles.▼

The sea is always moving. The **tide** comes in and out twice a day. As the waves break on to the shore they wear away the rocks and pebbles, changing the coastline all the time.

▲ These children are collecting shells and pebbles. Lots of people go to the seaside for their holiday. Have you been to a beach? What did you see on the shore when the tide went out?

Lots of sand

Deserts are open, empty places. They can be very hot during the day and very cold at night. There is very little soil in the desert and it hardly ever rains.

Some deserts are covered with sand which the wind has rubbed away from the rocks. The wind blows the sand into large piles called sand dunes. This means that the shape of the desert changes all the time. Other deserts are just bare rock.

Only a few kinds of animals and plants can survive in the desert because there is very little water. Cactus plants can grow because they have long roots that go deep down into the ground to find water. They also have special leaves that store water.

Most people who live in deserts move around from place to place, like these people who live in the desert in Iran. ▼

Plains

Plains are very wide, flat areas of land. Millions of years ago they may have been sea or lake beds, but now the water has gone.

Some plains have very good soil. Other plains are not so fertile and only grass and bushes will grow. The soil of the Prairies in the USA and Canada, is very good for growing wheat. ▼

Wild animals like lion, zebra and elephant live on the Serengeti Plains in Africa. ▶

These people are cattle farmers. They are called **Masai** and they live on the plains of Africa. They move around with their cattle to find new grazing ground. ▼

Changing the landscape

Deep under the ground there are many **natural resources** such as coal, tin, oil and iron. We need these resources to make many things, such as petrol, that we use in our everyday lives.

People build **mines** to dig these resources out of the ground. When a mine is built, the landscape is often changed as the earth is dug out and moved. This mine is in Wales. ▼

Some resources, such as oil, are deep under the sea, in the sea-bed. Huge oil-rigs are built so that we can drill down to get the oil out. ▲

Activity

Investigate resources that come from the ground. Can you find out what is made from these resources?

Building new landscapes

▲ Roads are built to make travelling quicker and easier, but as they are built, the natural landscape is changed. Sometimes whole hillsides are moved to make way for a new road.

People are building new landscapes every day. As more and more people are born, we need new houses, new factories and new roads and railways.

▲ Forests are cut down to make space for new houses and factories, or for farmland. When this happens, the natural landscape can be destroyed and may be polluted.

When we change the landscape we also change the **habitat** of the animals that live there. Some may be driven away and some may even die.

Investigate a local **building development** with an adult. What changes is it making to the landscape?

Landscapes for the future

Our world is a very special and beautiful place to live in. We have to learn how to take care of it. Many parts of the world are being changed by the ways in which people are using the land. How we plan and build new towns, how we grow food and how we find resources, all change the landscape around us.

▲ Sometimes the changes are carefully planned to improve an area. These gardens have been built to improve the landscape.

What kind of place would you like to live in? Look around the place where you live. If you were a **town planner**, how would you change the landscape to improve the area you live in?

Glossary

Boundary Where two countries meet.

Building development An area where new buildings are being made.

Channel A groove or passage in the Earth's surface that water may flow along.

Desert A large area of very dry, bare land where nothing much grows.

Face A steep side of a mountain.

Habitat An area that provides a home for a group of plants and animals.

Hollow A wide hole in the ground.

Landscape The shape and features of the land.

Masai The name of a group of people who live mainly on the plains of the Masai Mara in Africa.

Mine A series of holes and channels that are dug in the ground, so that people can remove natural resources.

Mound A pile or heap of soil and rock.

Natural resources A supply of things we use in everyday life, such as coal, oil and gas, that are found in nature and not made by people.

Peak The pointed top of a mountain.

Ridge The place where two slopes meet along the top of a hill.

Spring A natural source of water that comes from under the ground.

Tide The continuous rising and falling of sea level caused by the pull of the Sun and the Moon.

Town planner A person whose job is to decide how and where new buildings will be built in a town.

Finding out more

Books to read

Oceans by John Baines (Wayland, 1992)

Life in the Desert by Lucy Baker (Two-Can, 1991)

Life in the Mountains by Catherine Bradley (Two-Can, 1991)

Life in the Plains by Catherine Bradley (Two-Can, 1991)

Making a Motorway by James Dallaway (Wayland, 1992)

Mapwork 1 by David Flint and Mandy Suhr (Wayland, 1992)

Deserts by Ewan McLeish (Wayland, 1992)

Life on the Coastlines by Roseanne Hooper (Two-Can, 1992)

Shorelines by Sally Morgan and Pauline Lalor (Simon and Schuster, 1992)

Rivers by Jenny Wood (Franklin Watts, 1990)

Mountains by Jenny Wood (Franklin Watts, 1990)

Picture acknowledgements
The photographs in this book were supplied by: Cephas 4 below, 18 above, 22, 29 below; Chapel Studios 23 above; Bruce Coleman Ltd cover, 4 above, 7 above, 15, 23 above, 27; Eye Ubiquitous 5 below and above, 18 below, 29 above; G.S.F. Picture Library 21; LINK 8 below, Oxford Scientific Films 12; Tony Stone Worldwide 6, 7 below, 8 above, 9 above, 13, 16, 17, 20, 25, 26, 28; Zeta 9 below, 10, 14, 19, 24.

Index

Africa 23
animals 21, 23, 27

beach 18, 19
building 26, 27, 28, 29

cactus plant 21
Canada 17, 22
Caribbean 18
cliff 18
coastlines 4, 18

dam 16
deserts 4, 20, 21

Europe 14

farmers 8
farmland 10, 12
forest 11, 27

hills 4, 8, 10, 11
houses 4, 7, 28

Iran 21

lakes 16

Masai 23
mines 24
mountains 6, 7, 8, 9
  Alps 8, 9
  Himalayas 7
  K2 6

natural resources 24, 25, 28

oil 25

Pakistan 6
plains 22,23
  Masai Mara 23
  Prairies 22
  Serengeti 23
pollution 27

reservoir 16
rivers 4, 12, 14, 15
  Mississippi 14
  Rhine 15
road 15, 25

sand 18, 20
  dunes 20
sea 4, 14, 18, 19
soil 13, 14, 22
spring 16

Thailand 15
tide 19

USA 14, 17

valleys 12, 13

Wales 24
waterfall 17
  Niagara Falls 17